A Crabtree Branches Book

Today's Stars

PATRICK MAHO

Samantha Bell

Crabtree Publishing
crabtreebooks.com

School-to-Home Support for Caregivers and Teachers

This high-interest book is designed to motivate striving students with engaging topics while building fluency, vocabulary, and an interest in reading. Here are a few questions and activities to help the reader build upon his or her comprehension skills.

Before Reading:

- *What do I think this book is about?*
- *What do I know about this topic?*
- *What do I want to learn about this topic?*
- *Why am I reading this book?*

During Reading:

- *I wonder why...*
- *I'm curious to know...*
- *How is this like something I already know?*
- *What have I learned so far?*

After Reading:

- *What was the author trying to teach me?*
- *What are some details?*
- *How did the photographs and captions help me understand more?*
- *Read the book again and look for the vocabulary words.*
- *What questions do I still have?*

Extension Activities:

- *What was your favorite part of the book? Write a paragraph on it.*
- *Draw a picture of your favorite thing you learned from the book.*

TABLE OF CONTENTS

MVP

Patrick Mahomes began his football career in a big way. In 2018, just his second year in the National Football League (NFL), he became the **starting quarterback** for the Kansas City Chiefs.

MAHOMES
CHIEFS
adidas
adidas

Two years later, in 2020, Patrick led his team to Super Bowl LIV. The Chiefs were up against the San Francisco 49ers. They defeated the 49ers by a score of 31 to 20. It was the team's first Super Bowl since 1970.

Fun Facts

Each year, a player is chosen for the NFL Most Valuable Player (MVP) Award. Patrick won the MVP Award in 2018 and 2022. He was the Chiefs' first player to win the award.

FAMILY SUPPORT

Patrick Lavon Mahomes II was born in Texas on September 17, 1995. His father is Patrick "Pat" Mahomes Sr. and his mother is Randi Martin. Patrick also has a younger brother named Jackson.

Patrick with his family at the Super Bowl

Pat Sr. was a pitcher for several Major League Baseball (MLB) teams. The family traveled a lot when Patrick was small.

Pat Sr. as a pitcher with the Texas Rangers in 2001

Fun Facts

Pat Sr. tries to go to every game Patrick plays. He has sent the same message before every game since Patrick was eight years old. It says, "Players make plays, and I love you."

SCHOOL SPORTS

In high school, Patrick played basketball, football, and baseball. He **excelled** at all three sports. But college coaches who came to see him play thought he would pursue baseball. After high school, Patrick was **drafted** by the Detroit Tigers baseball team.

Patrick decided to go to college instead. In 2014, he started attending Texas Tech University on a football **scholarship**.

Fun Facts

The summer before his junior year of high school, Patrick thought about quitting football. But his mom convinced him to stick with it since he liked football more.

Patrick played football and baseball his first two years. His coaches thought his future was in baseball. But Patrick left baseball his junior year to focus on football.

Patrick walks off the field with Texas Tech head coach Kliff Kingsbury after winning a game in 2016.

THE PROS

In 2017, Patrick decided to leave college during his senior year to enter the NFL draft. He was selected by the Kansas City Chiefs. Patrick did not play much his first year.

The Kansas City Chiefs selected Patrick with the 10th pick at the 2017 NFL Draft in Philadelphia, Pennsylvania.

In 2018, the Chiefs traded their starting quarterback, and Patrick took his place. That year, Patrick made NFL history. He was only the second quarterback to throw 50 **touchdowns** and 5,000 passing yards in a single season.

Fun Facts

In 2020, Patrick signed a contract to extend his time with the Kansas City Chiefs for another 10 years. At the time of the contract, he was the highest paid athlete in sports.

ON FIRE

Patrick has led the Chiefs to the Super Bowl in 2020, 2021, 2023, and 2024. In 2020, he won his first Super Bowl against the San Francisco 49ers with a score of 31 to 20. In 2021, the Chiefs lost 31 to 9 against the Tampa Bay Buccaneers. In 2023, the Chiefs beat the Philadelphia Eagles with a score of 38 to 35. They followed up in 2024 with another victory against the 49ers. Patrick's pass as the clock ran out in overtime helped the Chiefs win 25 to 22.

Fun Facts

Patrick won Super Bowl MVP (Most Valuable Player) in 2020, 2023, and 2024. This ties him with Joe Montana.

As Patrick was building his football career, he was also building a **reputation**. Patrick is known for keeping his cool, especially in close games.

Patrick is also known for his creative and difficult throws. They include a left-handed pass and a **no-look pass**. Patrick practices every throw, since he knows he may make them during a game. He credits his unusual throws to his training in baseball.

A BRIGHT FUTURE

In March 2022, Patrick married his high school sweetheart Brittany Matthews. They have two children, a daughter named Sterling Skye and a son named Patrick "Bronze" Lavon III.

Fun Facts

Patrick's daughter received a scholarship offer from Texas Tech before she was a month old. She was offered a spot on their soccer team in 2039.

Patrick uses his **notoriety** to help make a difference. He appeared in a Black Lives Matter video. He joined basketball player LeBron James in helping increase **voter registration**.

LeBron James

VOTE
TODAY!
I MATTER. YOU MATTER. WE MATTER.
BLACK VOTERS MATTER
BlackVotersMatterFund.org

In 2019, Patrick launched the 15 and the Mahomies Foundation. This organization supports programs for kids that focus on academics, the arts, athletics, after-school programs, and more.

Patrick Mahomes is one of football's biggest stars. His talent and hard work have helped him rise to the top.

GLOSSARY

drafted (DRAFT-ed): Chosen to play on a professional sports team

excel (ek-SEL): To perform better than others

no-look pass (NOH LOOK PAS): A pass made without looking in the direction the ball travels

notoriety (no-tuh-rai-UH-tee): Being famous for something

reputation (rep-yoo-TAY-shuhn): The general belief or opinion that people have about someone or something

scholarship (SKOL-er-ship): Money given to a student to pay for their education

starting quarterback (STAAR-tihng KWOR-ter-bak): The leader of a football team's offense

touchdown (TUHCH-down): The act of scoring 6 points in football by catching or carrying the ball across the other team's goal line

voter registration (VOH-ter reh-ju-STRAY-shun): The process by which citizens become eligible to vote in elections

INDEX

WEBSITES TO VISIT

https://www.15andthemahomies.org

https://www.chiefs.com/team/players-roster/patrick-mahomes

https://kids.kiddle.co/Patrick_Mahomes

ABOUT THE AUTHOR

Samantha Bell lives with her family in the foothills of the Blue Ridge Mountains. She has four gray cats with a lot of attitude. When she's not writing, she likes to draw, hike, and visit new places.

Crabtree Publishing

crabtreebooks.com 800-387-7650

Written by: Samantha Bell
Designed by: Kathy Walsh
Series Development: James Earley
Proofreader: Melissa Boyce
Educational Consultant: Marie Lemke M.Ed.
Production manager: Candice Campbell

Hardcover: 978-1-0398-3907-6
Paperback: 978-1-0398-3992-2
Ebook (pdf): 978-1-0398-4064-5
Epub: 978-1-0398-4136-9

Printed in the U.S.A./CP2025

Published in Canada
Crabtree Publishing
616 Welland Ave.
St. Catharines, Ontario
L2M 5V6

Published in the United States
Crabtree Publishing
347 Fifth Ave
Suite 1402-145
New York, NY 10016

Library and Archives Canada Cataloguing in Publication
Available at Library and Archives Canada

Library of Congress Cataloging-in-Publication Data
Available at the Library of Congress

Photographs: Shutterstock, Newscom: Cover, Title pg, Backgrounds: Maria Lysaker@Newscom, Anna Davidovskaya, StockAppeal, Vector Tradition, Miloje; p 5, 6, 19, 29: StockAppeal; p 7, 11, 14, 19, 21, 25: Vector Tradition; p 3: William Purnell/IconSportswire; p 4: Robin Alam/ Icon Sportswire; p 5: Erik Williams; p 6, 7: John Angellillo; p 8: Rainer Lesniewski; p 9: Kevin C. Cox; p 10: Spencer D. Cook/"Ai Wire Photo Service"/Newscom; p 11: David Eulitt; p 12: Andrew Dieb/Icon Sportswire; p 13: Matthew Pearce/Icon Sportswire; p 14: Christopher Brashers/Icon Sportswire; p 15: Richard W. Rodrigues; p 16: Rich Graessle/ Icon Sportswire; p 17: John Mersits; p 18: Scott Winters/ Icon Sportswire; p 19: Nick Tre. Smith/Icon Sportswire; p 21, 21: Scott Winters/Icon Sportswire; p 22: Ken Murray/ Icon Sportswire; p 23: Nick Tre. Smith/Icon Sportswire; p 24: Jamie Lamor Thompson; p 25: John Angelillo; p 26: Kevin C. Cox; p 27: Erik Williams, Michael Scott Milner; p 28: JoeSAPhotos, Monkey Business Images; p 29: William Purnell/Icon Sportswire; p 31: Scott Winters/Icon Sportswire